ISLANDS OF THE PACIFIC RIM

AND THEIR PEOPLE

Robert Macdonald

Wayland

PEOPLE
· AND PLACES ·

The Alps and their People

The Amazon Rainforest and its People

The Arctic and its People

The Ganges Delta and its People

Islands of the Pacific Rim and their People

The Mediterranean and its People

The Prairies and their People

The Sahara and its People

Front cover: Loading and unloading goods on a beach of black volcanic sand.

Title page: For centuries fishing has provided a staple food for the islanders of the Pacific Rim. Here Indonesian fishermen cast nets off the coast of Flores Island.

Contents page: Tribal dancers on New Guinea and nearby islands create spectacular effects with their costumes using the plumage of native birds.

Series editor: Paul Mason
Designer: Mark Whitchurch

First published in 1994 by Wayland (Publishers) Ltd
61 Western Road, Hove, East Sussex, BN3 1JD, England

© Copyright 1994 Wayland (Publishers) Ltd

British Library Cataloguing in Publication Data
Macdonald, Robert
   Islands of Pacific Rim and Their People.
   – (People & Places Series)
I. Title II. Series
990

ISBN 0-7502-1214-4

Typeset by Dorchester Typesetting Group Ltd
Printed and bound in Italy by G. Canale & C.S.p.A.

Picture acknowledgements

The artwork was provided by Nick Hawken (page 4) and Peter Bull (pages 12 and 21).
The publishers would like to thank the following for allowing their photographs to be used in this book: Chapel Studios/Tim Garrod 9, 22, 39, Mary Evans 8, 24, 25; Eye Ubiquitous cover, contents page, 5, 6/7, 10, 14, 15, 16/17, 37, 40, 41, 42, 45; Hutchison 31 (T Motion), 33 (R Lloyd); Image Select 23, 26 (Archiv fur Kunst und Geschichte), 28, 28/29; Impact 18 (M Henley); Oxford Scientific Films 13 (KB Sandved), 19 (W Cheng), 43 (M Pitts); Popperfoto 30; Survival Anglia 35 (M Pitts); Tony Stone Images 32 (A Sacks), 34 (P Seaward), 36, 38; Topham 27, 44.

CONTENTS

A Ring of Fire   4

Forests   9

Ocean   16

Colonialism   22

Pacific War   26

The Economic Miracle   30

Problems of Prosperity   35

Destruction of the Rainforest   40

Future Issues   43

Glossary   46

Books to Read   47

Useful Addresses   47

Index   48

· A · R I N G · O F · F I R E ·

The volcanoes that surround the Pacific Ocean are often described as the Ring of Fire. A map of the region shows them dotted all the way up the eastern coastlines of South, Central and North America. They loop across the top of the Pacific Ocean, creating the necklace of volcanic islands called the Aleutians. Then the volcanoes continue down the western edge of the Pacific. They are found rising above the surrounding countryside on the large island groups lying off the coastline of the continent of Asia.

Volcanic activity helped create and shape these formations of islands on the western rim of the Pacific. They include Japan in the north; the Philippines and the Indonesian archipelago which lie further south, in the warmer seas off the land-mass of Southeast Asia; and Papua New Guinea which is just north of Australia.

An archipelago is a sea with many islands or a collection of islands, and Indonesia is the largest archipelago in the world. It is also the largest nation in Southeast Asia. There are more than 3,000 islands making up the Indonesian Republic – 17,508 if you count all the small islets. They stretch along the Equator over a distance of 5,120km. On these islands there are more volcanoes than anywhere else in the world, including 178 that are still active.

Altogether there are thousands of volcanoes in the Ring of Fire. Many are believed to be extinct (they are no longer active and dangerous). But all around the Pacific there are many that are still smoking and others that are dormant. That means they are sleeping and unpredictable. In some areas no one can be sure when or where the next explosion will happen.

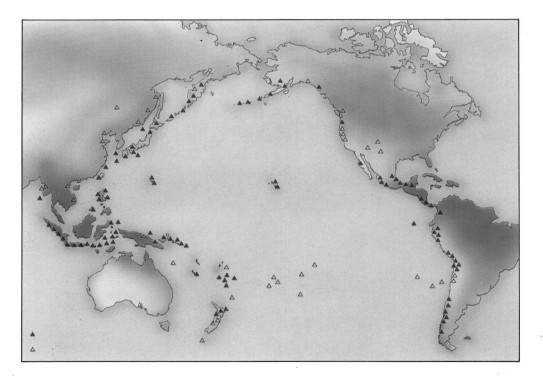

◄

This map shows the volcanoes of the Pacific Ring of Fire. The filled-in red triangles are active volcanoes, the empty ones are extinct volcanoes.

Mount Bromo, on the Indonesian island of Java. The mountain is considered sacred, and pilgrims journey to view magnificent sunrises from Bromo's summit.

The Ring of Fire is especially active, alive and dangerous in Indonesia and the Philippines. A volcano called Mount Pinatubo erupted in the Philippines in 1991. It sprayed so much dust into the upper atmosphere that the climate of much of the world was altered temporarily. Less heat from the sun reached the earth's surface because of the ash cloud, and people blamed Pinatubo for cold summers in both the southern and northern hemispheres.

One of the most densely populated parts of Indonesia is the large island of Java, which has 95 million inhabitants. They live mostly on the plateau in the centre and the fertile plain on the northern side of the island. Along the southern coast is a belt of volcanic mountains. There are 121 volcanoes in this belt including 27 which are active. They are a danger to the population but they also bring the island wealth. As volcanic rock decays it produces extremely fertile soils. In this part of the world the land surrounding volcanoes is often highly populated. People risk the dangers of eruptions and earthquakes because they make such a rich living from the land. On Java the lower slopes of many volcanoes are shaped into intricate terraces for growing rice, and on many other islands people work the soil in the shadow of smoking volcanic cones.

Why is there a Ring of Fire around the Pacific, and why is volcanic and earthquake activity so intense among the islands of the Pacific Rim, from Japan in the north to Indonesia and Papua New Guinea further south? Only in this century have we begun to understand something of the forces that produce chains of volcanoes.

The world's continents are all in a state of very slow movement, drifting apart from one another or coming closer together. The outer surface of the globe is made of a hard crust of rock. The crust, like an eggshell, encloses deeper layers of the earth called the mantle. The mantle is also made of rock but deep below the surface this becomes semi-molten and almost fluid. On the surface the world's crust is divided like a jigsaw puzzle into plates which rest on the treacly mantle beneath them. It is along the edges of these plates that volcanoes and earthquakes are common.

Seven major plates and a number of smaller ones divide up the crust. When plates pull apart from each other they leave a gap which allows molten rock to rise to the surface from the earth's mantle. This happens often on the sea-bed, spreading the sea-bed and pushing the continents further apart. Sometimes islands are created by the cooling rock.

Terracing for rice, tea and other crops in a dangerous landscape – the fertile soils of a volcano on the island of Java.

When plates collide one plate is pushed beneath the other, and as it sinks the rock from the earth's surface becomes molten again. The molten rock, pushing its way through the earth's crust, may create 'necklaces' of volcanoes along the collision line

and there may be deep trenches in the ocean floor where one plate has plunged downwards.

In Southeast Asia and the south-eastern Pacific area four major plates are jostling up against each other now. The Ring of Fire around the Pacific follows plate boundary lines. Along these lines earthquakes are frequent too: Japan holds the record. In one year in the city of Gifu there were 516 earthquakes detectable without instruments. Tokyo, the capital city, averages about 150 each year. In 1923 the most destructive earthquake in Japanese history killed 100,000 people and destroyed over 300,000 buildings. It was centred on Sagami Bay south of Tokyo, and lifted parts of the coast by nearly two metres. Among the islands of the Pacific Rim the physical world is still in a constant state of movement, change and collision.

*The tidal wave which followed Krakatoa's eruption in 1883 swept large craft inland.
This paddle-steamer was beached many kilometres from the coast of Sumatra.*

Over the centuries volcanoes have brought natural disasters to Indonesia and the Philippines. In 1815 Tambora on the Indonesian island of Sumbawa exploded. The eruption was so violent that the top half of the volcano was blown away, reducing it from 4,300 metres to a mere 2,800. Many thousands of people died from the blast or from the gases and debris that smothered their villages.

Another 82,000 died later from disease and starvation, having lost fields and crops.

Many were killed also by huge tidal waves which swept over the low-lying land soon after the eruption. These waves created by the shock of volcanic explosions are called by a Japanese name, tsunami. In the Western Pacific giant tsunami often accompany volcanic eruptions, causing devastation.

There was another terrible volcanic eruption in Indonesia in 1883, when the small island of Krakatoa, in the Sundra Straits, was blown apart. So much magma (molten rock) was blown out that the remains of the island collapsed into a great hole which was then filled by the sea. Giant tsunami were created. They swept over the coastal plains of West Java and the island of Sumatra, killing many thousands of people.

· F O R E S T S ·

JAPAN

*T*hough volcanic forces have shaped them, the islands of the Pacific Rim have very different personalities. Japan has a climate that ranges from cool and temperate in the north to sub-tropical in the south.

It is said that there are six seasons in Japan. This is because China and the whole continent of Asia lies close by, across the Sea of Japan. The great Asian landmass warms in summer and cools in winter, regularly sending fronts of warm and cold air backwards and forwards over Japan: these bring heavy monsoon rains in June and a shorter spell of rain at summer's end. Thus there are two rainy seasons as well as the normal spring, summer, autumn and winter.

Rugged mountains cover 80 per cent of Japan. They shield the Pacific coast of the main island of Honshu from the freezing winter winds blowing from Siberia and Manchuria. Many of the mountainsides are covered in forests. In fact Japan has more land covered in forests – 60 per cent – than any other industrialized nation outside Scandinavia. There are forests of subtropical evergreen hardwoods such as cedar in the south. Further north, there are forests of deciduous trees, such as the oak, beech and ash which lose their leaves in winter; and forests of fir and spruce on the colder island of Hokkaido, farthest to the north.

The people of Japan live tightly packed together on the narrow strips of coastal land.

▲
Japan's great variety of forests includes deciduous trees like these providing a colourful autumn display at Nagatoro.

Amazingly, despite the lack of space, Japan has the world's seventh largest population – just over 125 million people.

Because of the mountains only a small amount of land can be farmed – 15 per cent – but more is grown per hectare than anywhere else in the world. Rice is the most important crop and Japan grows enough to feed itself. Other cereals and many other foodstuffs have to be imported, however. Strangely enough, Japan also imports more wood than any other country in the world, even though forests cover so much of its mountain country. Much of this timber comes from the island groups to the south – the Philippines, Indonesia and Papua New Guinea.

The forests to be found in these island groups are very different to those in Japan. In the Philippines, in Papua New Guinea and on the Indonesian islands of Sumatra, Java, Sulawesi, Kalimantan (the Indonesian part of Borneo) and Irian Jaya (Indonesian New Guinea) there are large and small areas of tropical rainforest.

RAINFORESTS

Rainforests are the natural vegetation of much of Southeast Asia but they are rapidly disappearing in many places. They have largely gone from many islands and a number of mainland countries, but Southeast Asia remains one of three great rainforest areas (the others are West Africa and South America).

Tropical rainforests grow where there are high average temperatures and high rainfall. They are the oldest type of forests on earth and have the greatest variety of plants, animals, birds and insects. They extended across most of the world 45 million years ago. Nowadays the rainforests cover less than two per cent of the globe, yet they have living in them between 40 and 50 per cent of all living things – five million different kinds of plants, animals and insects.

In a temperate forest in Europe or North America there may be only eight species of tree in each hectare, but tropical rainforests can contain dozens of different species in the same area.

For tens of millions of years the Southeast Asian climate has suited rainforests, and there is an even greater richness of plant-life there than in South America and Africa. The great variety of plants and animals is partly a result of the volcanic eruptions, earthquakes and rising sea-levels which have broken up the land and created so many islands. In each separate area, over the years, species have evolved in a different way from their close relatives over the mountains or on the neighbouring islands.

A rare tiger on the Indonesian island of Java. The tigers live deep in the rainforest, where the trees provide them with shade and cover.

'Emergent' trees tower above lower tree-levels in this tropical rainforest in Kalimantan, on the island of Borneo.

Many thousands of years ago, when the Ice Age lowered sea-levels around the globe, there was a land bridge linking the western islands of Indonesia with the Southeast Asian mainland. Many large animals were confined to particular islands as sea-levels rose again. Sumatra has its own variety of rhinoceros and tiger, and a big ape, the orang-utan, found elsewhere only on neighbouring Borneo. There are many other animals – monkeys, wild cats, squirrels, deer – in the western islands of Indonesia, related to species found in Indochina and the rest of mainland Asia. However, animals, birds and plants all change as you travel eastwards to islands which have never been joined to Asia.

In these eastern islands animal and plant life is linked not with that of the Asian mainland but with Australia to the south. Cockatoos related to those of Australia, and animals similar to Australian marsupials (mammals with pouches in which the young are born and reared) are found on Indonesian islands such as Sulawesi and the Maluku group.

There are different levels to the rainforest. The high canopy is where most animal and bird life is found. This is where the crowns of the tall trees join together in a continuous forest roof of leaves and branches, and where in the heat of the equatorial zones there are flowers and fruits all the year round. Birds and climbing mammals such as

◄ Bali and Lombok were thought in 1856 to be 'The extreme points of two great zoological divisions' by Alfred Wallace. In 1902, the line was replaced with Weber's Line, and it has subsequently been argued over by many zoologists.

An Orang-utan. The near-human personality of Sumatra's great ape led to its name, which means Man of the Forest.

the monkeys and apes feed on these fruits. The canopy may be 45m in height: above it rise isolated 'emergent' trees. Southeast Asian emergents are taller than those of other rainforests and they can reach 70m.

Despite being tremendously tall, forest trees often have very shallow root systems, taking their nutriment not from deep in the ground but from the leaf-litter of the forest floor. The first Western explorers and botanists who travelled through the rainforests did not realize the significance of this. They thought the abundant life of the tropical forests meant they grew on very rich, fertile soils. In fact rainforest soils can be very poor. Special fungi on their roots help many trees absorb minerals and water efficiently, but they gain most nourishment from the decaying matter of the forest itself.

A way forward for the forest

The international timber industry has a bad record of ruthlessly exploiting rainforests. Often overseas companies pay local people little for the timber which the forest people own, and even avoid paying taxes or a fair rate for logging licences to the countries in which they operate.

In 1992 a newspaper in Papua New Guinea (PNG) reported that up to forty timber companies were operating there without proper environmental plans, and some were believed to be logging without permits. Local tribespeople, with no understanding of business in the outside world, are unable to gain a fair deal or stop their forests being destroyed.

A new way forward for the forests and the local people is being tried out by the Ecological Trading Company (ETC), formed in Britain in 1989. The company's aim is to develop a trade in tropical timber that will benefit local people and not destroy the natural environment. There are now community schemes in South America and also in PNG, in which local people carry out small-scale logging without the use of heavy machinery. Timber is sawn up in the forests and the whole community, including women, join in carrying the planks to the nearest point of collection. Everybody gets paid a fair rate for this work. Some timber is used locally, and the ETC finds a market overseas for the rest of the wood.

A woman of the Dayak tribe gathers medicinal herbs in Belega Forest, Sarawak, on the island of Borneo. Western medicine is only now beginning to discover many valuable plants in the rainforest.

A waterfall plunges over crags on the island of Bougainville, Papua New Guinea. Such beauty is currently threatened by logging activities.

There have been few other success stories in stopping rainforest destruction. Timber is not the only resource being lost. In 1990 Friends of the Earth organized a conference in London on The Rainforest Harvest. Speakers talked of many natural products including oils, nuts, mushrooms, herbs and spices, honey fruits and root crops, and medicines. In the West one of the most feared diseases is cancer, and scientists believe a cure could be found in the rainforests. They have identified three thousand plants worldwide which could help fight cancer, and 70 per cent of them come from the rainforests.

In the Milne Bay Province of PNG a number of community groups have acquired portable mills and done training courses in timber working. They have exported container loads of mixed hardwoods to the ETC in Britain. In the future there may be many more companies in the West co-operating with tribespeople in a fair trade for rainforest products as the message of conservation spreads.

· O C E A N ·

*T*he ocean has always been of enormous importance to all the island peoples of the Pacific Rim. Throughout Southeast Asia there are many communities whose people are as much at home on the sea as on land. The best known are probably the *orang laut* – the sea people or sea gypsies – who are found throughout Southeast Asia, from the coast of Burma to the Philippines. They make a living from the sea and spend their lives on family boats. On tropical islands such as New Guinea and Borneo there are many tribespeople who build their houses on stilts out over the water on coastal bays and estuaries. When the tide is in you can obtain dinner

▶
There are spectacular undersea gardens and a rich variety of marine life in the waters round Indonesia, and these Balinese fishing boats are a few of those which harvest the seas.

without leaving home, by dropping a fishing line from the verandah.

Fish are an important part of their diet for many Pacific Rim people, including the Japanese, who nowadays have a fleet of more than 430,000 registered fishing boats. They sail all over the Pacific on fishing expeditions, going as far south as New Zealand and beyond, into the waters of the Southern Ocean and Antarctica. The Japanese eat their fish both cooked and raw, and a famous dish is *sashimi* – finely cut slices of raw fish served with green horseradish (or you can have *sushi* – slices of raw fish on carefully shaped mounds of vinegared rice).

There are even restaurants in Japan which specialize in cooking a highly poisonous species of fish. Only a small part of this creature can be eaten: if the chef is not expert at cutting away the rest the customer dies.

Japan's fishing industry

The Japanese diet is very different to that of most Western countries. The Japanese eat few milk and dairy products such as cheese and butter, and much less meat than people in America or Europe. But fish and shellfish are very important foods for them, and they eat more of these than any other nation. There are rich fishing grounds around Japan's coasts though problems arose at the end of the Second World War. The USSR occupied islands north of Hokkaido and took control of the routes leading to Japan's fishing grounds in the Sea of Okhotsk. Since then many new sources of fish have been found and the Japanese have pioneered fishing technology, using electronic devices to locate fish shoals. Every year 1 million tonnes of fish and shellfish are cultivated in fish farms, on top of the 13 million tonnes caught by Japanese fishermen.

Fresh tuna is an important fish especially for dishes such as *sushi* and *sashimi*. Nowadays much of the tuna is caught in Indonesian waters. The Indonesian town of Muara Baru has become an important fishing port, developed with financial aid from Japan. Taiwanese, South Korean and Japanese fishing boats use the port and tuna is sent by air from there to Japanese tables. Japanese boats travel to many parts of the Pacific, and Japan is also the major customer for fish products from countries as far to the south as New Zealand.

The fish market at Tsukiji in Tokyo. Japanese people eat more fish than most others, and Japan's fishing industry is very important to the life of the country.

Whales and dolphins, many varieties of shark, shoals of tuna and thousands of varieties of spectacularly coloured fish are at home in the waters of the Pacific and the seas around the Southeast Asian islands. In tropical waters there are coral reefs where the underwater life is almost as rich and diverse as the ecosystem of the rainforest. Many of the extinct volcanoes of the Pacific Ring of Fire have become, over thousands of years, coral atolls. Volcanic cones are heavy and gradually they sink beneath the sea, but as they do so coral grows around the cone. Its growth keeps pace with the sinking and eventually all that is left of the volcano is a circle of coral rising a few feet above the waves, usually crowned with coconut palms.

Below the waves is a rainbow-coloured wonderland of coral gardens alive with swaying marine plants, strange-shaped coral flowers, darting fish and occasional turtles.

It was this richness of marine life that, perhaps six or seven thousand years ago, encouraged people to set out from the South China coast to find new homes on the many islands out to sea. They may have settled first on the island of Taiwan (also called Formosa) which lies south of Japan. Some moved on from Taiwan to the Philippines and Indonesia, island-hopping in dugout canoes. As their skills of seamanship, navigation and canoe-building developed over centuries, these emigrants from the mainland moved further out into the ocean. Today around the tropical islands of the Pacific Rim and across the Pacific you can still find the same type of craft as they used. These are canoes with outriggers (wooden floats lashed to poles projecting from the side of the canoe that improve its balance).

Modern language studies show us that the peoples of the Malay Peninsula, Indonesia, the Philippines and the Polynesian islands of the Pacific are all closely related. Together they are known as the Austronesians or Malaya-Polynesians. Probably they are descended from those early voyagers who left the South China coast to explore the seas. In early times no other people spread so far and crossed such vast expanses of ocean. The region of the Pacific Rim is an ideal area for seafaring people to develop their skills. Volcanic activity has created chains of small islands which lead like stepping-stones from one large island group to the next. The Southeast Asian rainforest provided food, plants and animals that could be transported from island to island – root crops like the yam and taro; trees and palms like the coconut, breadfruit and banana; and live creatures – the dog, pig and jungle fowl. These were all carried far across the Pacific.

When they first settled the tropical islands of the Pacific Rim the Austronesian voyagers came across groups of people already living on the islands, whose origins were quite different to theirs. They had darker skin and curly hair. They had been on the islands a very long time – since the last Ice Age in fact. In Southeast Asia land bridges linked many of the islands to the Asian mainland or to Australia during the ice ages. People were able to travel by land across the region.

This other group of people who arrived much earlier than the Austronesians we call Australoids, and there are still large populations of them. They include the Australian Aborigines, the Papuan tribespeople of New Guinea, the Melanesian islanders and groups of tribal people still to be found in the Philippines and elsewhere in Southeast Asia, known as the Negritos. Though many of them reached their present homes by land there must have been some who used canoes or even rafts to cross wide stretches of open water.

The sea surrounding the Pacific Rim islands has traditionally been a source of life, in the form of food, but it has also been a source of danger and death. Tsunami, terrible tidal waves, sweep across low-lying land after volcanic eruptions and earthquakes. Another danger in the region is typhoons – fierce tropical storms which blow in from the sea at speeds of up to 200 km/h. The north-west Pacific in particular is a breeding ground for typhoons. Between July and November Japan suffers especially, but at various times they can bring devastation to all the Pacific Rim islands.

From early times the seas have also been highways for invaders from elsewhere. The Indonesian archipelago guards the route from the Indian Ocean through to the China Seas and the Pacific. Hundreds of years ago traders began to visit the Indonesian islands, bartering for spices and other goods. So famous were the spices that the islands became known as the Spice Islands.

Nowadays Indonesia is the largest Muslim country in the world: Arab traders converted many of the Spice Islands to Islam seven hundred years ago. Before that Buddhism and Hinduism had spread from India and great temples were built. The island of Bali remains a stronghold of Hinduism, while Christianity and animism are both practised by tribespeople on Irian Jaya – the Indonesian half of New Guinea.

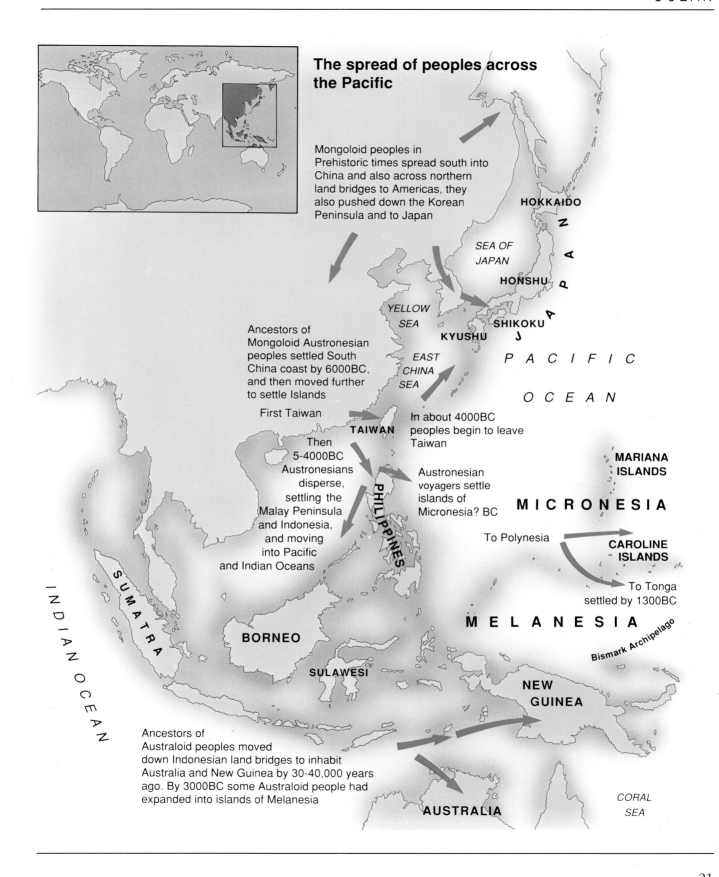

The spread of peoples across the Pacific

Mongoloid peoples in Prehistoric times spread south into China and also across northern land bridges to Americas, they also pushed down the Korean Peninsula and to Japan

HOKKAIDO

SEA OF JAPAN

HONSHU

J A P A N

Ancestors of Mongoloid Austronesian peoples settled South China coast by 6000BC, and then moved further to settle Islands

YELLOW SEA

KYUSHU

SHIKOKU

First Taiwan

TAIWAN

EAST CHINA SEA

P A C I F I C

O C E A N

In about 4000BC peoples begin to leave Taiwan

Then 5-4000BC Austronesians disperse, settling the Malay Peninsula and Indonesia, and moving into Pacific and Indian Oceans

Austronesian voyagers settle islands of Micronesia? BC

MARIANA ISLANDS

M I C R O N E S I A

PHILIPPINES

To Polynesia

CAROLINE ISLANDS

To Tonga settled by 1300BC

M E L A N E S I A

Bismark Archipelago

S U M A T R A

I N D I A N   O C E A N

BORNEO

SULAWESI

NEW GUINEA

Ancestors of Australoid peoples moved down Indonesian land bridges to inhabit Australia and New Guinea by 30-40,000 years ago. By 3000BC some Australoid people had expanded into islands of Melanesia

AUSTRALIA

CORAL SEA

·COLONIALISM·

EARLY TRADERS

Nowadays we use the word colonialism mainly to describe what happened when the seafaring nations of Europe began to seize and control territory overseas, in America, Africa, Asia and the Pacific. In Asia when the first European travellers went to trade with the local peoples for products such as spices, silks and porcelain there was often fierce rivalry between Portuguese, Spanish, English, Dutch and Arab expeditions. Each country tried to get a trade monopoly and keep out its rivals. In the Spice Islands of the Indonesian archipelago Islamic traders from Arabia were at first so powerful that they kept out all European shipping, until in 1511 a small Portuguese fleet attacked and conquered Malacca, the most important trading port in the Orient.

Among Europeans there was a belief that Christianity was the only true religion. Traders took priests with them and converted and baptized hundreds of islanders. The Spanish and Portuguese – the first colonialists – thought it was their duty to wage holy war against infidels (an Arab word for those who do not share the same religious belief as you). But greed was mixed up with religion, and conquered territories were exploited for their wealth. Many local people lost their freedom and were made to do forced labour in the mines or on the land.

▶ *Indian traders took Hinduism and Buddhism to Southeast Asia centuries ago, and great temples were built. The face of the Sri Mahamarianman Temple in Kuala Lumpur, Malaysia, is decorated with gods and mythic figures from Indian legend.*

Magellan and the Spanish Empire

The great navigator Ferdinand Magellan led a Spanish expedition to the Philippines in 1521, and he died there, killed in a battle with a local chieftain. Only one of his five ships managed to struggle back to Spain, but it has a special place in history – the first ship to travel round the globe. During the next 60 years the Spaniards sent further expeditions, gradually taking control of the islands.

Spanish galleons began sailing regularly between the islands and Mexico. For 250 years these huge 'wooden-walls' sailed across the Pacific carrying fabulous cargoes of silks and gems, porcelain, sandalwood chests, spices and ivory, to be sent on to Europe. Silver ingots and chests of silver and gold coins were carried back as payment. They were dangerous voyages. Galleons were lost in typhoons, and attacked by pirates. An English sea captain called George Anson captured a galleon in 1743 and sailed back to London with its cargo. Thirty-five carts were needed to carry the treasure away from the docks.

FERDINAND MAGELLANUS.

◄

Magellan led Spanish ships to the Philippines and died there in 1521.

HOLLAND AND ENGLAND

As the northern European countries developed their shipping fleets they joined in the scramble for trade and possessions. Holland had become a great trading centre and in northern Europe there was enormous demand for eastern spices – pepper, cinnamon, cloves, nutmeg. In 1602 Dutch merchants banded together and formed the United Dutch East India Company to try to take over the spice trade.

The Dutch were to prove even more ruthless than the Portuguese in the East Indies. The Dutch East India Company was given the power by Holland's government to raise armies and wage war. Gradually they gained control of most of the Indonesian archipelago. Dutch rule was to last for nearly 350 years. To stay in power they fought two great wars on the island of Java. The second war between 1825 and 1830 led to the death of 200,000 Javanese and 8,000 Europeans.

The English were also aggressive colonizers and established their own trading posts in the East, including the great port of Singapore on an island at the tip of the Malay Peninsula. From there they occupied Java for a brief period in the 19th century.

The European scramble for colonial possessions reached its climax in the 19th century. On the Pacific Rim the large island of New Guinea was divided up between the Dutch, the Germans and the British. The tribespeople were not asked if they wanted this to happen. The USA too become a colonial power in the region in 1898. During a short war with Spain the USA captured the Philippines, and held on to them for the next 43 years.

Dutch settlers took control of the East Indies and imposed their rule by war. Many of them then began to live lives of great luxury – this man is being carried around so that he doesn't have to walk in the heat – while the local people became very poor.

***Commodore Perry's Black Ships
came to Japan in 1853 and forced the country to open trade with the West.***

JAPAN

Of the large island nations close to mainland Asia, only Japan was able to keep her independence during the years when European ships were roving the China Seas, seeking trade and also territories to control. Being a long way from most trade routes, Japan was able to use the ocean as a barrier, to keep the outside world away. In the early 17th century the rulers of Japan were worried by the increasing influence of traders and Christian missionaries from Europe. They closed the country, expelling foreigners and forbidding Japanese to travel overseas. For 264 years Japan remained hidden. Only a few Dutch and Chinese merchants were allowed to trade. Their ships were kept isolated in a small part of the port of Nagasaki. Then in 1853 a squadron of warships appeared off the coast, commanded by Commodore Matthew Perry of the US navy. The Japanese called his fleet the Black Ships.

For many years Western countries had been asking Japan to open its ports to their ships. The USA had particular reasons for wanting this to happen, for it was starting a regular mail service between California and China. Steamships were to be used and they cannot travel far without stopping to get more coal. The USA wanted the ships to be able to stop in Japan for coal and supplies.

Faced with Commodore Perry's Black Ships and their modern guns, the Japanese were forced to agree to abandon isolation and to accept once more visitors and traders from the rest of the world.

· P A C I F I C · W A R ·

Japan changed dramatically between 1853 and the start of the twentieth century. Many Japanese were eager to learn about Western scientific discoveries. Some Japanese went overseas to learn about heavy industry in the West – engineering and shipbuilding. The rulers who had kept the country isolated were removed and Japan began a period of rapid modernization. The aim was to catch up with the West; to equal the strength of the Western nations.

By the beginning of the twentieth century Japan had developed a navy powerful enough to defeat both the Chinese and the Russian navies. It also built up a modern army; so war-like that it soon became a threat to both the West and to Japan's Asian neighbours. Japan's government was not able to control the army effectively. Some army officers saw how European nations had empires overseas, and believed that a strong Japan should rule over Asia. In 1931 they began a campaign to seize China's northern provinces – an area called Manchuria.

Eventually Japan's ambitions to rival the West were to lead to a war engulfing the

A Japanese submarine at Port Arthur in 1904. By then Japan had begun to create a modern navy, and was trying to expand into Korea and Manchuria. This brought conflict with Russia, and the Japanese fleet defeated the Russians at Port Arthur. A year later they were defeated again, at Tsushima, and the war ended in September 1905.

The Japanese emperor

Emperor Mutsuhito of Japan in 1901.

Among the island nations of the Pacific Rim Japan is the only one with a monarchy – the oldest unbroken monarchy in the world. The present Emperor, Akihito, is said to be a descendant of the Emperor Jimmu Tenno who, it is claimed, reigned in the seventh century BC.

Legend shrouds Japan's early history and the origins of its emperors. The royal family claimed the sun-goddess Amaterasu as their earliest ancestor, and the emperor was looked upon as a living god until the end of the Second World War. Then the US occupation force insisted that he renounce all claims to be a god. He is now the symbol of the state but has no governing powers.

In fact for much of Japanese history the emperor had little real power, though he played an important part in the fertility rituals of the earliest religion of his people, Shinto. For hundreds of years the real power in Japan was held by military leaders, called Shogun, supported by the samurai or warrior class (about six per cent of the population). The last Shogun was overthrown by reformers under the Emperor Meiji in 1868.

whole Pacific. Having taken Manchuria the Japanese army began fighting to take control of the whole of China in 1937.

To fight a modern war you need materials such as rubber and oil. These were available on the Malay Peninsula and in Indonesia, then still called the Dutch East Indies. Japan is a country with few natural resources of its own, and as fighting continued the military leaders needed to find resources elsewhere.

The European colonial powers were too busy fighting the Second World War against Germany to defend their Asian territories properly. Japan wanted the Southeast Asian colonies controlled by Britain and the Dutch and French: Malaya with its rubber plantations, the port of Singapore, Burma, Indo-China (now Kampuchea, Laos and Vietnam), the Dutch East Indies, even India.

The Japanese military rulers saw that the only strong force that could stop them in the Pacific was the US Pacific fleet of battleships. The US fleet was based at Pearl Harbour in Hawaii. Japan decided to remove this threat to dreams of military conquest. On 7 December, 1941, Japanese planes attacked the fleet. They sank or badly damaged eight battleships.

This was the start of the Pacific War which during the next four years brought misery to all the islands of the Pacific Rim. Japan's powerful forces swept down the Pacific and the Asian mainland after their attack on Pearl Harbour, winning victory after victory against the British and Americans. They captured the Philippines after fierce fighting, and took the British stronghold of Singapore.

Victims of the Allied atomic bomb attack on Hiroshima, in hospital. In the years after the attack, many thousands died of radiation poisoning.
▼

Japan dreamed of leading the rest of Asia in a struggle against the West – its territories were called the Co-Prosperity Sphere. But Japan's armies treated the other peoples of Southeast Asia and China so brutally that few supported them. As the USA and her allies regained strength Japan could not hold on to the vast area she had conquered. Gradually her forces were pushed back up the Pacific by US, British and Australian forces. There were terrible battles at sea and on small coral islands. Japanese soldiers fought to the death and kamikaze pilots flew suicide missions, deliberately crashing their bomb-laden planes on enemy battleships. At the same time, Japan's cities were bombed by US aircraft. In August, 1945, with the country on the brink of defeat, the USA dropped its new weapon

on the Japanese city of Hiroshima. This was the first atom bomb. Three days later another atom bomb was dropped on the city of Nagasaki. Japan surrendered a few days later. The country had lost between two and three million young men who had been killed in its struggle to rule the Asian world. Many of its heavily populated cities – Tokyo, Nagasaki, Hiroshima, Osaka – were in ruins.

US troops advance on the island of Bougainville, in 1944. The Pacific War devastated some islands, destroying towns and cities, and stopping farmers from planting crops.

· THE · ECONOMIC · MIRACLE ·

Yokohama, 1945: an iron safe is all that is left of the contents of a house.
But with US aid, Japan was soon to become an industrial giant.

At the end of the Pacific War there was devastation on many of the islands of the Pacific Rim. Japan's capital city, Tokyo, and many of her other cities were in ruins. In the Philippines the capital, Manila, had suffered severe bombing. Even in Papua New Guinea the war left its mark, with sunken ships blocking harbours and crashed planes in the rainforest. Some small Pacific islands where fierce battles took place were left a wasteland of shell-holes and destroyed vegetation.

Colonialism could not survive in most of the Pacific Rim countries after the war. The Dutch were weak after their wartime experience of Nazi occupation. They tried to return to the Indonesian archipelago but found there was a nationalist revolution there (nationalists want their countries to be ruled by the local people and not by other nations). In 1950 the Dutch finally left and the Spice Islands of the Dutch East Indies gained a new name – the Republic of Indonesia. For another 13 years the Dutch held on to their half of the island of New Guinea, but in the end United Nations pressure led to this territory being handed over to Indonesia too. It is now called Irian Jaya.

The Philippines also gained their independence from the USA a year after the war, and could rule themselves at last.

For seven years after the end of the Pacific War US forces controlled Japan, heading an Occupation Force. Their job was to turn Japan from a militaristic country into a peaceful democratic nation.

Some Western governments wanted to remove all Japan's heavy industry so it could never fight a war again. Events in China persuaded the USA not to do this. There was a civil war in China after the Japanese left, won by the Chinese communists, who took over the government in 1949. The USA feared communism would spread, and decided a prosperous Japan could be an ally against communism. US money repaired Japan's factories.

Reforms were made by the Occupation Force. Land was distributed to the people who worked on it. The education system was improved. Factory management was modernized. When in 1951 the USA found itself at war again, fighting the communists in Korea only 160 kilometres from Japan, Japanese industry was asked to provide materials for the US forces – iron and steel, army lorries, cement, clothing.

Probably no other country has ever recovered so quickly from wartime destruction as did Japan. It was partly due to direct US help and partly to the war in Korea bringing work to Japan's factories. It was due also to the skill of the Japanese and their government. They put all their profits and their energies into buying the most modern equipment for their factories and finding new peacetime products to develop and market.

A busy urban street on the Indonesian island of Sulawesi. After the destruction brought by the war, the Pacific Rim began to rebuild itself. Now it has one of the fastest-growing economies in the world.

All these things led to what has become known as the Japanese economic miracle. From 1954 onwards the country's economy kept growing by 10 per cent each year. Japan just kept on getting richer.

By the 1980s the Japanese were earning more than any other people in the world. They had overtaken even the USA. The secret of this success lay in the modernization of their industry, and in their skill in developing and improving other people's inventions. For instance in 1953 a small Japanese electronics company called Sony bought from the USA a licence to develop a new piece of technology. With this they made the world's first transistor radios and soon were selling them all over the world.

No other country makes such a large range of electronics goods as does Japan – personal stereos, radios, televisions and video recorders, cameras, computers and telecommunications devices are all exported and sold around the world.

The island of Taiwan has also grown rich since the war. Like Japan its development was carefully planned and its people worked hard. Taiwan has not been a centre of highly modern industry: instead it produced cheap goods such as plastic toys and sports shoes for overseas markets. But now, like Japan, Taiwan is concentrating on high technology and moving towards its own economic miracle.

Taiwan's road to prosperity began in 1949 when the island became the refuge of Chiang Kai-shek and his followers. Chiang was leader of the Nationalist Chinese forces, who fought against the Japanese during their occupation of China. He was elected president of the Republic of China after the war, but soon afterwards his Nationalist army was defeated on the mainland by rebel Chinese communists, who had also fought the Japanese. The Nationalists fled to Taiwan and set up a government again, claiming still to be the true rulers of all China.

A Japanese car worker. Japan's automobile industry is the envy of the world, producing well-made, reliable vehicles in some of the world's most modern car assembly plants.

High-rise office blocks and roads crowded with traffic in Jakarta, the capital of Indonesia. Just as Japan did in the 1950s and 1960s, the other Pacific Rim nations are emerging as powerful economic forces.

The communists set up a government in Peking (now Beijing), and called themselves the People's Republic of China. They were not accepted at first by the Western nations, and China's seat in the United Nations went to the rival government on Taiwan. US aid went to Taiwan too, and the businessmen who had accompanied Chiang on his flight from the communists began the process of building up the economy and industry of the poverty-stricken island. Much support from the West was withdrawn in 1979, however, when the United Nations changed its mind, and recognized the communist government's right to represent all the Chinese people in international politics.

The Taiwan Chinese still claim the whole of China, and the communists on the mainland look upon the island of Taiwan as part of their country.

Cars and Pollution

Japan's motor-vehicle industry (cars, buses, trucks) is now the world's largest. The Japanese car firms Nissan and Toyota are two of the top three car makers in the world, and they have built factories overseas as well as in Japan. To build these cars they have created complex machines, which do the boring repetitive jobs that used to be done by people. Japan has more of these industrial robots than all the other developed countries in the world combined. Highly skilled and educated workers control them.

The success of Japan's motor industry has a serious down side. The centre of a major Japanese city, especially Tokyo, is often blocked by traffic jams in which people can sometimes be stuck for hours without moving. The long lines of cars with their engines running produce exhaust fumes that rise up into the atmosphere and create a layer of smog, like those found in cities such as Los Angeles and Athens.

The post-war wealth of Japan is partly to blame for this problem, and so is Japan's peaceful attitude. Before the war the country was not so wealthy, and much of the government's money was spent on armaments, so few people could afford cars. Now Japan has grown rich. Its constitution does not allow it to have an army and the government invests in industry instead. These factors combine to mean that almost all Japanese can now afford a car.

Central Tokyo: trains at two levels, and the streets are clogged with traffic.

▼

·PROBLEMS·OF· ·PROSPERITY·

South Korea, Singapore and Hong Kong are small nations which have been called Asia's 'economic dragons'. Like Japan, they have all prospered in recent years by developing high-tech industries and trade. Taiwan has joined the dragons now, and the Pacific Rim region is leading the world in economic development.

Pollution colours a still corner of the harbour in Hong Kong, one of Asia's 'economic dragons'.

As well as new wealth, this brings many problems to the region. The most obvious is pollution. Japan's rapid industrial development during and after the Pacific War brought terrible consequences. By the late 1960s Japan was probably the most polluted country in the world, because of the way factories had been built in and around the major cities. There had been no attempt to control the pollution from the factories: the bay around which Tokyo stands was so poisoned that fish could hardly survive in its waters. The waste from oil refineries, chemical plants and steel mills, and Tokyo's sewage all went into the bay. It was said in 1971 that there were so many chemicals in it that film could be developed in the bay water.

Some of Japan's most famous beauty spots have been destroyed by this pollution. The lovely Inland Sea lying between two of Japan's main islands, Honshu and Shikoku, became one of the world's most contaminated seas. It was once a rich source of seaweed, a favourite item of Japanese diet, fish and shellfish. Suruga Bay, south of Tokyo and overlooked by Japan's famous mountain, Fujiyama, was considered one of the most beautiful places in Japan until it was choked by industrial waste from four huge paper mills.

Pollution has poisoned the atmosphere of many cities, too. Photochemical smog in Tokyo is caused by car exhausts and factory chimneys, and falls of metal dust and black rain have created alarm in Japanese cities. There have been worse consequences for many people. In 1953 fishermen's families in Minamata, a village on the coast of the island of Kyushu, were struck down by a mystery disease. People who ate local fish and shellfish began suffering from muscular spasms, and there were cases of blindness. Babies were born with brain damage. It was found that a local aluminium factory was pouring deadly waste containing methyl mercury into the bay, and this was the cause of what became known as 'Minamata disease'. In other parts of Japan there were similar tragedies, caused by factories polluting their surroundings with cadmium waste, arsenic and other poisons. There are serious pollution problems in Taiwan too, and on all the Pacific Rim islands where there has been rapid and uncontrolled industrial development.

▲
A sugar mill in the Philippines. The sugar industry often pays low wages, and its workers may be very poor.

Rubbish and rainwater create a stench in a Surabaya back-street, East Java. Although many of the islands have a thriving economy, most of the people of the cities live in poor housing and earn very low wages. The new wealth of the islands is not shared equally between all their inhabitants.

Some islands, like Java in Indonesia, are over-populated and this brings many kinds of environmental damage. The neighbouring island of Bali suffers from what might be called tourist pollution. Bali, a beautiful island, has always attracted visitors fascinated by its untouched traditional ways of life and its rich culture. There has been an explosive growth of tourism recently, however, and many who come to the island have little interest in its traditions. Thousands of Australian holiday-makers want a cheap vacation on a tropical sea-shore, while thousands of Japanese come simply to play golf on one of the hundreds of golf courses.

In South Bali the lovely coastline with its ancient villages is being transformed with the building of golf courses, landscaped parks for tourists, marinas and tourist villages built cheaply of cement breeze-blocks.

Tokyo

Japan began as a rice-growing country in which everyone joined together in the work of building terraces for the rice crop and irrigating the fields. Such work has to be done by a whole community. This tradition of living and working as a group continues in the crowded modern world. People are not as individualistic as they are in Western countries but they are very polite to each other. There is very little street crime in Tokyo, the capital of Japan, even though it is Asia's largest and most prosperous city, and the most expensive place in the world to live (twice as expensive as New York).

It is a city that has been destroyed many times, by fire, by earthquake and by fire-bombs during the Second World War. As a result there are few old buildings to be seen. There has been constant building activity since the war, and the city is always changing. It sprawls across a bigger area than any other city in the world, and around it are bed cities, which are enormous suburbs. People

Evening lights transform downtown Tokyo, home to about a quarter of Japan's population.

Many pedestrians in Tokyo and other cities wear face-masks to guard against pollution and bacteria.

commute from these to work in Tokyo.

The commuter trains are so crowded that on station platforms there are men called *shiri-oshi*, which means bottom-pushers. They wear uniforms and gloves. As the crowds squeeze into the trains their job is to push the last people aboard, so the doors can close.

Tokyo was originally a castle city, built round the stronghold of the Shogun who ruled Japan. The castle is sill there, rebuilt since the wartime bombing. Now it is surrounded by an urban sprawl of crowded roads, industrial buildings and high-rise office blocks designed to withstand earthquake shocks. There

was little planning in the city's rapid development after the war. It is probably most attractive when seen at night when there is a spectacular display of city lights and dramatic neon signs.

About a quarter of Japan's population jostles for space in the Greater Tokyo area. This is one reason why the cost of living is so high. Housing is extremely expensive and apartments are often small. In compensation for the cramped conditions at home there are many eating and entertainment places in most neighbourhoods and communal bath-houses too. Men often return home late, eating out with their work colleagues or with clients.

Women in Japan are normally married by the age of 25. Many stay at home and see little of their husbands who often work extremely long hours. *Shafu* – company spirit – is very important, and men may be expected to give up their free time for the company which employs them. Death from overwork is so common that a new word, *karoshi*, has been invented to describe it.

At school Japanese children have to work very hard too. There is great pressure on them from an early age to pass tests and to get into the best secondary schools. There is an expression used about school in Japan – *shiken jigoku* – which means examination hell. The rules of behaviour for children are strict and most girls and boys wear uniforms to school. These are often old-fashioned and military in style – sailor blouses for girls and dark jackets for boys with brass buttons and stand-up collars (the boys must often wear their hair cropped, like army cadets of former times).

·DESTRUCTION·OF·THE·RAINFOREST·

One serious problem facing the region is the rapid destruction of much of the rainforest. This is not happening just in Southeast Asia. Rainforests have been disappearing quickly during the last 30 years all over the world. Friends of the Earth, an environmental charity which campaigns against environmental damage, estimates: 'Every second of every day an area of rainforest the size of one football pitch is being destroyed.' On the tropical islands of the Pacific Rim many forest trees are being cut down for export to overseas buyers, particularly Japan. Japan takes more than half (and Europe more than one quarter) of all the world's wood exports. Tropical hardwoods are popular in fine furniture-making but wood from millions of tropical trees is also used in building and in paper-making.

Nowadays Indonesia gains a large portion of its export earnings from selling timber. Only the sale of oil brings more money into the country. In 1968 timber sales were bringing the Philippines a third of all their earnings from overseas, but the forests have been so heavily logged that the sales nowadays are much smaller. A recent report said the state of the forests in the Philippines was probably the worst in Asia, because of heavy logging and other damage.

▶ *Members of the Penan tribe sit on logs from their territory in Sarawak. The Penan are a tribal people at home in the rainforests of Sarawak, Malaysian Borneo, but their forest homeland is being ruined by logging.*

Logs from Kalimantan are loaded aboard a ship on Sulawesi. They are probably destined for Japan, where they will be used in the construction industry.

In Papua New Guinea forests have been heavily logged too, and hundreds of thousands of tonnes of logs have been sent to Japanese paper-making factories.

The problem of logging is that in many areas the forest never recovers. Roads are built and heavy machinery used to pull logs from the forests. The vegetation surrounding the trees is killed, the soil damaged and the delicate balance of forest life is destroyed. Roads made for timber trucks attract settlers, who clear away the remaining forest to make farmland. Gradually the rainforest is pushed back. Sometimes logging companies promise to re-plant the forest, but often they plant eucalyptus trees which are quick to grow, not the slow-growing tropical hardwoods. Eucalypts or gumtrees do not provide native wildlife with food, and birds and animals disappear with the rainforest trees.

Throughout the world people are worried about the destruction of the rainforest because we do not know the value of what we are losing. A large number of valuable drugs and medicines have come from rainforest trees and plants, and there are many more still to be discovered. Important food plants have first been discovered in the rainforests, including rice, bananas, pineapples, cocoa and brazil nuts. The aboriginal peoples who live in the rainforests know many more food plants and some of these could become valuable crops for farmers elsewhere.

There is such a wide variety of species in Southeast Asian forests that only a small portion has been studied by scientists. Any small section of forest can possibly contain unique trees and plants that are found nowhere else. If this forest is cut down these will be lost for ever.

A cargo cult ceremony on Papua New Guinea. Members of cargo cults often believe that in the future the ruin of their homes will end and they will once more be rulers of their lands.

The rainforests are home to many tribal peoples too, and their societies are destroyed with the forests. We are only just beginning to realize how valuable are the lessons these people have to teach us. For thousands of years they have learned how to gain food and medicinal herbs from the forests and how to grow crops without damaging their environment. They know far more about the forest than anyone else. In the Philippines there is one forest tribe called the Hanunoo who divide the plants in their territory into 1,600 categories. This is 400 more than botanists know.

In Indonesia government policy has had a disastrous effect on many rainforest areas and tribal peoples. Because of over-population on islands such as Java it was decided in the 1950s to encourage Indonesians to migrate to the outer islands: Sumatra, Kalimantan (the Indonesian section of Borneo), Sulawesi and Irian Jaya (the western half of the island of Papua New Guinea). This Transmigration Programme has sent almost two million people to the outer islands to turn the forests into farmlands. As a result of the Programme, tribal peoples have lost their land and wild animals have lost their habitat. The inexperienced settlers have caused soil erosion and flooding by stripping trees from hillsides and clumsily clearing the land of its covering. The soil then becomes less fertile.

· F U T U R E · I S S U E S ·

Huli warriors from the Central Highlands of Papua New Guinea. Western football jerseys and bird-of-paradise feathers make their costumes.

*F*ew regions of the world offer such great contrasts in life-styles as does the Pacific Rim, where nations range from the high-technology culture of Japan to the Stone Age culture still to be found in modern times on the island of New Guinea. Nowadays this island is divided in two; the western half controlled by Indonesia and the eastern half the independent state of Papua New Guinea.

The artificial line dividing the island is a reminder of the region's colonial past. It could be a source of future problems, for since Indonesia took over its half of the island from the Dutch there has been resistance from tribespeople to Indonesian rule. A Free Papua Movement organized guerrilla attacks on Indonesian troops in the 1980s.

Papua New Guinea is still busy turning itself into a cash economy (where people use money instead of bartering for the goods they cannot provide themselves). Here is another problem, for although you need money in Papua New Guinea to buy food or to pay tax, there are very few jobs available for people who leave their villages to live in the towns. As a result there are gangs of men who are called 'rascals', who have turned to crime to gain cash.

The most violent place in the region is not Papua New Guinea, however. It is the small island territory of East Timor. This was formerly ruled by Portugal but Indonesia took control by force in 1976. Indonesia has been at war with East Timorese fighters for independence ever since. Some estimates say almost a third of the island's population has died in the fighting. Indonesia allows no outsiders to visit East Timor, so no one can know for sure.

February, 1986: demonstrators against the Philippine dictatorship of Ferdinand Marcos are hosed with water cannon and beaten by police. Marcos was expelled from the Philippines and later died, but his wife Imelda has now returned.

Since Indonesia became independent there have been a number of violent upheavals on the main islands. Political freedom is strictly controlled by President Suharto's government (he gained power after a military coup in 1965).

Politics have been unstable and sometimes violent in the Philippines too, since independence. Ferdinand Marcos was elected president in 1965, and when his time as president was up he declared martial law and stayed on. He and his wife Imelda used their power to accumulate wealth. When the couple were forced to flee the country in 1986 it was said they had taken five billion dollars (£3.3bn) from the economy. Imelda has now returned to the Philippines as a politician.

By contrast with its wartime record, Japan has been the most peaceful of the Pacific Rim island countries since 1945. Many other Asian countries look to Japan nowadays as a model for their own development in the future. For Japan the big question is whether the economic miracle can be made to continue, or whether there are harder times ahead. Because of high costs and higher wages in Japan, industrialists are building their new factories in the other poorer countries of the Pacific Rim these days. In Japan itself people are increasingly aware of the problems of pollution. Hopefully those problems will not be exported and the Pacific Rim countries will learn from past mistakes and begin to cherish their environment once more.

New Guinea body decorators

The island of New Guinea is split down its length by a massive mountain range, with peaks reaching over 4,000 metres. In these highlands are many valleys that are home to tribes isolated from the rest of the world for thousands of years, all with their own particular language. There are more languages spoken in New Guinea than anywhere else in the world – over 700 in fact. Many of the highland tribespeople are famous for their body decoration, making use of coloured earths to paint their skin and creating spectacular head-dresses from the plumage of birds and other materials. They are helped by the fact that New Guinea has some 1,500 different birds including 38 varieties of the bird of paradise – the gaudiest birds of all. Nowadays when the painted and decorated warriors assemble for some festival they attract photographers from around the globe. Because of the huge number of languages spoken in New Guinea, Pidgin English developed as a form of communication. This simple language takes most of its words from English but includes German and tribal words. 'Good morning' is moning, 'good afternoon' apinun, 'thank you' is tenkyu and 'food' is kaikai (restaurant is haus kaikai).

A painted warrior from the New Guinea Highlands. Body painting with coloured earths is common among the tribal peoples of New Guinea, Australia and Melanesia.
▼

Aboriginal Existing in a place from the earliest known times. The aboriginal peoples of the Pacific Rim are the descendants of the first peoples who lived there.

Animism The belief that objects and animals contain souls.

Archipelago A collection of islands.

Atoll A circular coral reef or a string of coral islands that surround a lagoon.

Australoids The descendants of the early voyagers who left the south China coast to explore the western Pacific.

Austronesian The descendants of the earliest settlers in the western Pacific, who came from Australia and Southeast Asia.

Cargo cult When isolated tribespeople in New Guinea and Melanesia first saw aircraft arrive from the sky, bringing rich cargoes to white traders and missionaries, they thought that by magic and ritual they might also persuade the gods to send them heavenly cargoes. Mock aircraft and airstrips were built in the rainforest, and ceremonies were held to entice aircraft from the clouds. These ceremonies continue today in various forms.

Colonialism Expansion by one country so that it governs territories outside its own borders. The term is most often used to describe the expansion of sea-going European powers, especially in the nineteenth century.

Coral Hard, rock-like material created in patterned formations by millions of small sea-creatures called marine polyps. The material protects them and forms their support on the sea-bed. Gradually it accumulates to form small islands.

Developed country A country with a large economy, and good health care and education systems.

Economic dragons The Southeast Asian states with the most powerful economies: South Korea, Singapore and Hong Kong.

Ecosystem A group of plants, animals and soils that are all dependent on each other for their survival.

Fertile Rich or fruitful: a fertile piece of land is one on which a larger than average amount of a crop will grow.

Monsoon A time of especially heavy rain, often brought by winds from the south-west.

Natural resources Things from the natural world that can be turned into manufactured items: rubber trees, for example, are a natural resource that can be turned into car tyres.

Papua New Guinea An independent country made up of the eastern half of New Guinea and nearby islands (among them the Bismark archipelago, the west Solomon Islands and the Trobriands). From 1949 until 1975 the country was ruled by Australia.

Plateau A large, flat region of land, often raised up above the level of the surrounding area.

Shinto The earliest religion of Japan, Shinto believes in living in harmony with nature, recognizing spiritual forces in the natural world (in some ways it resembles **Animism**).

Spice A pleasant-smelling or powerfully aromatic

plant substance used for flavouring food. Pepper and cloves are spices.

Temperate Mild in climate: neither hot nor cold for much of the year.

Tsunami A giant wave caused by an undersea earthquake. Tsunami is a Japanese word made up of two others, *tsu* (port) and *nami* (wave): a tsunami is a wave large enough to make even a normally safe port dangerous.

Typhoon A violent storm of very powerful winds, also called a cyclone. The name comes from the Chinese words *tai* (great) and *fung* (wind).

·BOOKS·TO·READ·

Coral Reefs of the World: Central and Western Pacific World Conservation Union/United Nations Environment Programme, 1988.

An Empire of the East – Travels in Indonesia Norman Lewis (Jonathan Cape 1993).

The Guiness Guide to the Restless Earth – the Landscapes of our Planet and the Forces that Shaped them Professor KJ Gregory (editor) (Guiness Publishing 1991).

Kingdoms of the East – Animals of the Orient Colin Willock (Boxtree/Anglia TV, 1991). The book of a TV series.

Life in the Rainforests – Animals, People, Plants Lucy Baker (Two-Can 1990).

New Guinea – An Island Apart Neil Nightingale (BBC Books 1992).

In the Rainforest Catherine Caulfield (Picador 1986).

·USEFUL·ADDRESSES·

International
For advice on the situation of tribal peoples:
International Work Group for Indigenous Affairs
Fiolstraede 10
1171 Copenhagen K
Denmark

For information on the marketing of rainforest products:
The Body Shop International
(Marketing Rainforest Products)
Watersmead
Littlehampton BN17 6LS
Britain

Malaysia
Biology Department
Universiti Kebangsaan
Malaysia 43600
Bangi Selangor
Malaysia

Indonesia
Dr Otto Soemarwoto
Padjajaran University
Bandung
Indonesia

Numbers in **bold** show
where text is accompanied
by a photograph.

animal life, east-west
    division **13**
Arab traders 22
atomic bomb 29

Black Ships **25**
Bromo, Mt **5**

cargo cults **42**
colonialism
    Dutch and English 24
    Portuguese and Spanish
    22, 23
    post-war death 30

earthquakes 7
East Timor 44
'economic dragons' 35
economic recovery,
    post-war 31, 32

farming, on volcanic soil
    6-**7**
fishing **1**, 17, 18, **19**

Hiroshima, atomic bomb 28
Hong Kong, pollution **35**

Indonesia 4, 8, 24, 30, 43-4

Bali 37
Java 5, 24, 37, 42

Japan
    automobile industry **32**,
    33
    emperor **27**
    expansion of power in
    twentieth century 25, 26-7
    fishing industry 17, 18
    forests **9**-10
    isolationism 25
    war with Russia, 1904 26

land rights of forest people
    41-2
logging **10**, **40**-1

Manchuria 26-7
Magellan **23**

Orang laut (sea gypsies)
    16-17
outrigger canoes 19

Papua New Guinea 15, 24,
    42, **43**
    body decorators **45**
Philippines 23, 24, 30, **36**,
    42, **44**
    demonstrations **44**
    Marcos, Ferdinand and
    Imelda 44

pollution
    air 34, 36, **39**
    industrial 36
    ocean **35**, 36
    tourist 37

rainforests *see also* logging
    10-**11**, 13, **14**, **15**
    preservation 14-15
religion 20, 21
Ring of Fire **4**-7

spice trade 20, 22, 24
spread of peoples across
    the Pacific 19, 20, **21**
Sulawesi **31**
Surabaya, Java **37**

Taiwan 19, 32-3, 35
Tokyo 38-9
tsunami 8, 20

volcanoes 4, **5**, 6
    formation 6
    Krakatoa 8
    Tambora 8

Wallace Line **12**
Weber's Line **12**

Yokohama, wartime
    destruction **30**